The Internet Marketing Secrets 101: How to write killer copy to influence and persuade people to buy almost anything you sell

By Malik Johnson

©2017 WE CANT BE BEAT LLC

Copyright 2017 by Malik Johnson.

Published by WE CANT BE BEAT LLC

Krob817@yahoo.com

Table of Contents

This page is intentionally left blank 9

Introduction 10

Chapter 1 - Website design 17

Chapter 2 - Communication - The secret to effective internet marketing 23

    Search engine optimization 25

    Pay-per-click (PPC) search marketing 26

    Online Public relations 28

Chapter 3 - Understanding the consumer mindset for writing mind-blowing copy 30

    Reading the mind of your customer 33

    Web browsing history 35

Chapter 4 - Copywriting – from essential to critical to vital 37

    From machine language to being human 37

    Keep it simple not clever 38

    What is simplicity in copywriting? 39

    Chopping down the message to bare essentials 40

    The giraffe 41

Chapter 5 - Tricks in writing a great sales page which will sell your product like hot cakes 51

    Tips for Creating Effective Landing Page Which Converts Like Crazy 52

Tips for Planning the Layout of Your Landing Page 59

The nuts and bolts of a landing page 64

Chapter 6 - Swipe files and how to do it the right way....68

Chapter 7 - The sales funnel 74

Let your customers land softly on your website....75

Sales funnel revisited 78

Chapter 8 - Affiliate programs 82

What is an affiliate program? 82

The benefits of an affiliate program........................83

How does an affiliate program work? 86

Chapter 9 - Highest paying affiliate programs 89

Amazon Affiliate program..93

Clickbank...94

CJ Affiliate..94

eBay affiliate program 95

ReviMedia..95

Chapter 10 - Email marketing - getting close to the customer 97

Designing effective email newsletters 102

Chapter 11- Viral marketing...104

Emails as a viral channel 107

PR sites as viral channels 108

Facebook and Twitter 109

Chapter 12 - Social media marketing 111
   Facebook marketing 112
   Twitter marketing 114
   Bookmarking 114
Conclusion 116

☐ Copyright 2017 by Malik Johnson - **All rights reserved.**

This document is geared towards providing exact and reliable information in regards to the topic and issue covered. The publication is sold with the idea that the publisher is not required to render accounting, officially permitted, or otherwise, qualified services. If advice is necessary, legal or professional, a practiced individual in the profession should be ordered.

- From a Declaration of Principles which was accepted and approved equally by a Committee of the American Bar Association and a Committee of Publishers and Associations.

In no way is it legal to reproduce, duplicate, or transmit any part of this document in either electronic means or in printed format. Recording of this publication is strictly prohibited and any storage of this document is not allowed unless with written permission from the publisher. All rights reserved.

The information provided herein is stated to be truthful and consistent, in that any liability, in terms of inattention or otherwise, by any usage or abuse of any policies, processes, or directions contained within is the solitary and utter responsibility of the recipient reader. Under no circumstances will any legal responsibility or blame be held against the publisher for any reparation, damages, or monetary loss due to the information herein, either directly or indirectly.

Respective authors own all copyrights not held by the publisher.

The information herein is offered for informational purposes solely, and is universal as so. The presentation of the information is without contract or any type of guarantee assurance.

The trademarks that are used are without any consent, and the publication of the trademark is without permission or backing by the trademark owner. All trademarks and brands within this book are for clarifying purposes only and are the owned by the owners themselves, not affiliated with this document.

This page is intentionally left blank

Introduction

The entire world has moved online and those who haven't have become obsolete. The first mover's advantage has already been taken by smart organizations and businesses. This does not mean that others like you have lost out. The online market is huge and its potential has not been explored even fractionally. Many big businesses have moved online and are reaping its benefits. This does not mean that the internet is only for the big boys. Small businesses, niche players and individuals, in fact everyone is making merry online. Savvy brick and mortar marketers have grasped the importance of internet marketing and have developed unique and novel marketing techniques to attract buyers online.

By reading this book you will get access to some trade secrets which only a few internet marketers are privy to. You will learn how to develop a strong and effective internet marketing strategy. In addition we will explore some of the aspects in greater detail, like copywriting for the internet.

You, like many others, may be under the impression that marketing is same everywhere. Even established businesses with big brands have made this assumption and suffered. Internet marketing is as different from traditional marketing as apple is from oranges. You must behave differently online to catch the customer who is internet savvy and knows a trick or two to strike a good deal. Smart buyers visit traditional outlets, try and explore different products, but go online to buy because it is far cheaper and convenient. As a result, old-fashioned shopping malls have become trial rooms and experimental labs. This phenomenon is frustrating for businesses, but a great opportunity for smart internet marketers.

You need a new and novel business model to handle and manage your business on the internet. What does this model look like? How can you master the techniques to quickly capture your intended market? What skills and tools are required to take your business to the next level? This is exactly what you will learn from this book.

This book will take you through the different stages of internet marketing. You will learn how to acquire customers through search engine optimization and Pay per click marketing. Affiliate marketing is massive and humungous field which you must understand well. Small businesses and individuals have made millions through affiliate marketing. Online advertisements and PR can catapult you to unimaginable heights. Email marketing is another online channel to acquire customers.

Every marketer knows the issues associated with converting customers. You can take a customer to the lake but it's very difficult to make him drink the water. Customer conversion and retention are critical for your online business. This book will expose you to the tricks and ways to make customers buy into you. Content creation and content management is the key to success. You should know the art of writing compelling and creative copy. Website design and development should be given their rightful place in the marketing strategy. There is no point having a great product unless your target customer is made aware that such a product exists. Some businesses assume that simply creating a website is enough to get people flocking to them. It doesn't take time for them to realize that they are wrong. Online customers are picky and choosy. They don't like shoddy websites. Nobody wants to wait for web pages to download. Your customer is likely to move on to your competitor site if yours takes time to load. Website usability and accessibility are important factors to keep visitors stick to you and do not abandon your site.

The opportunities on the internet are immense but so are the challenges. The competition is fierce. Internet marketing is democratic, in the sense that you don't need deep pockets to sell online. As a result, for every one Goliath there are ten David's waiting to conquer the internet. Smart and savvy businesses can compete with the biggest brands and win. Don't you think internet is a huge prospect for you?

Selling on the internet is a different cup of tea - Tastier and sweeter. You should learn how to design sales pages which attract and compel customers to click the buy button. You must master the art of creating landing pages which can catch the big fish. This book will expose you to headline swipe files, sales funnels, online branding and many more secrets.

Your website is not the only place to sell your product. Email marketing compliments your other strategies. The social media is big business. Loyalty programs, gift vouchers, games and gifts form an important pillar of internet marketing.

Monitoring website traffic, estimating click-through rates, fine tuning the sales funnel and measuring various other parameters are necessary if you want your internet strategy to work. This book will take you through various stages of managing and monitoring your website.

There are many other recent additions to internet marketing. Video marketing is making waves and there is a massive demand for online videos. Mobile marketing has taken online marketing by storm. These developments are transforming online marketing scenario. Customers are now buying on the go. This has compelled marketers to focus on creating websites which can be accessed anywhere and anytime.

Ultimately, only those who adapt and change will survive the cut throat competition. Those who survive will reap unimaginable benefits. You must not only read this book but implement the strategies and put them into practice. Internet marketing is fun and a fantastic opportunity. This platform is open to everyone. You can find customers in Tokyo while sitting in Chicago. You can design products in Singapore, manufacture in China and sell in Mexico. The key to success is marketing because you will win only when you have customers.

Luckily you have now got hold of this book. You can learn everything about internet marketing here. This will serve as a comprehensive guide which will take you places. You must treat this book like a holy script and your prayers will certainly come true.

Chapter 1 - Website design

Effective web design does not mean using latest technology. It also does not mean bedazzling a customer with great graphics and visuals. It means the website should be able to generate profits for the business. The sole aim of a website is to attract, retain, influence and persuade a visitor to click on the buy button. Rest everything else is only secondary to this objective. You have to develop trust and convince the customer that you are genuine and offer the best in class products at the cheapest price. The customer must get the impression that you are offering a bargain which they should capitalize on immediately or they would miss a golden opportunity. Agreed that you can't please everyone – some may look for bargains while others may want to buy quality. This is where your business strategy comes into play. You have to first prioritize what you want your website to do, who are the prospective customers and what do they actually want. This can be quite a challenge. If you can resolve these issues you are well on your way to designing an effective website.

Your website will only be as good as the people who design it. Who are these people we are talking about? Of course we mean the internet marketers. You must employ a top down approach to website design which begins with the end user in sight and mind. Understanding the buyer or customer is the key to success. You should know exactly what kind of audience you website will be addressing. Some site may focus on high end, exclusive and expensive products like jewelry. Here the focus should be on providing the visitor with a personalized, tailored and a unique experience. Price is not an important factor. On the other hand, if you want your website to sell plastic buckets (which can be a fantastic online business by the way) the focus would be on durability and price. Website design is therefore based on the product which you want to sell. Understanding the customer in that particular marketplace in which you intent to operate is perhaps crucial to success. A detailed analysis of your competitor's site is an easy and dependable strategy. You can take a cue or two from competitors but it will be better if you can improve on them. Not every competitor is competent. It is possible that websites you are using as templates are poorly designed. Not every website is a model to be followed. The best option is to follow your own strategy while taking the best features from others.

Technically your website should be easy to access which means it should appear high up in search results, convenient to view with good download speed for web pages, should be easy to navigate and should provide ease of ordering.

You can use traditional marketing techniques to understand user requirements. Essentially you should be able to answer who, why and when of your customer. When evaluating usability of a website, you should discover why users leave your website and at what stage. Why and when prospective customers abandon your site will provide insights into designing an effective website. Your customer may abandon your site right on your home page which would be a disaster for you. This may happen because the customer cannot find what he came to find on your website. Customers may leave because your web page takes long time to download. Who has the patience to wait especially when other websites are only a click away? Site navigation may be another reason for customers to abandon your site. Confusing and complicated site design should be totally avoided. Customers may leave because they don't have enough confidence or faith on your payment gateway. What if someone steals their password and robs them of their hard earned money? Establishing your credentials by using security certificates is therefore essential. The worst part is that customers don't tell you why they abandoned your site. Zap and they are off to another portal. Website design should therefore take all aspects into consideration and leave anything to fate. Branding is another way to ensure that customers have sufficient trust in you to expose their credit cards to your payment gateway.

Importance of content in website design

You must have read that content is king. This is certainly true but only to an extent. There is good and bad content. Using flowery and difficult language (probably written by a graduate in literature) is bad content. Academic looking,, journalistic and high-flown language doesn't work when it comes to websites, unless your customers and professors and academicians.

The main page is the central piece of your website. The content here should b precise and objective – what do you offer on your website? Why should a customer buy from you? Which buttons to press to enable fulfillment? Should we use the word 'buy' instead of 'fulfillment'?

Content for the home page or for that matter the entire website should be concise. You are not writing a journal paper. Allow visitors to grasp the basics in one glance. You should use font sizes effectively to highlight the content. You should break down your text into small paragraphs. Remember that your customer is not reading from a book or a printed brochure. Viewing content on a computer monitor is stressful to the eye.

You should know that not all messages can be effectively conveyed through websites alone. You must use emails, messaging and even traditional voice calls to personalize your marketing. Websites are impersonal and they don't talk to anyone in particular. Customers would like specifics about a product which can only be delivered through other communication channels. Internet Marketing should therefore consist of various digital and traditional communication channels.

Chapter 2 - Communication - The secret to effective internet marketing

You need customers if you want to sell your product. Earlier, you could place ads in newspapers and magazines, go for television spots if you had the money, put up hoardings and do traditional PR to attract customers. Obviously you needed considerable amount of resources and money to undertake any of these activities. Off-line messaging had its advantages. Buyers had no option but to either go for you or your competitor's product. You only had to create a compelling copy and the rest was put on autopilot. There were no sticky questions and no need to answer them. You could push your product and depending on your budget you would have attracted the required audience. Brand building was the name of this marketing game and competition was limited. You should realize that technology has affected all industries. Earlier supply chain management used to be an issue. You needed huge amount of investment to maintain inventory spread over a vast geography. In such circumstances only the big players could survive and flourish.

Times have changed and how? Modern technology has changed the landscape. You can live and thrive with zero inventories. Distances have been shrunk by new transportation models and supply chains have been dramatically squeezed. The internet has revolutionized selling. The scenario has been altered beyond recognition. You need new and novel means of communicating with your customers. You have to understand the psychology of a different buyer who is likely to ask a hundred questions before nodding his head. Fortunately the cost of reaching the customer has come down considerably to the extent that even a small business can thrive online. Let's examine a few modern tools which you require to undertake an internet marketing campaign.

Search engine optimization

The phrase SEO does not need an introduction. By now it's a household term which has major implications in how you perform online. SEO or organic search was popularized by Google. Now search is synonymous with Google. Any internet marketer worth his salt has to understand the logic and meaning of search.

There is a mistaken belief that organic search is free. Oh, SEO is free, you will hear people say. They are wrong. Effective search strategy requires resources, money and creativity. Building traffic through SEO requires special skills which have to be mastered. Google may not charge you anything for ranking your site but they are quite choosy. There are numerous reasons why your website may find a place on the first page of search results or on the hundredth place. This book is on internet marketing and suffices to say here that SEO is one of the major pillars on which your strategy would stand. Search result pages of Google are the first place where your customer will touch base with you. Research has shown that seventy percent of your traffic will come from search. If you think that you will pay and buy traffic by using paid listings and banner ads, you have to think again. More than seventy percent of your traffic will come from free search. Users tend to choose the natural search results in preference to the paid search listings. You can guess why? The modern user does not rely on paid advertisements which they know can be gamed. You are now facing a smart and informed buyer who will hunt till he discovers your hidden skeletons if any. You can't fool this tech savvy gal who is already a master of making a good deal.

Pay-per-click (PPC) search marketing

Though not as effective as SEO, Pay-per-click (PPC) search marketing is another important tool for internet marketers. There are reasons why you may have to choose PPC campaigns.

You may be in a highly competitive market like insurance and a SEO ranking may not be easily gettable. Some websites may be using unethical means to capture search engine ranking using black hat SEO. You can't compete with such entities. Moreover your competitors may be saturating the internet with their banner ads creating high visibility.

There is one more limitation in organic search marketing. Your business will only appear in search results. What about other sites which may be relevant and bring traffic? In PPC, depending on the page content, you may be able to display contextual ads. You can play with the context by using different keywords and create text ads usually called 'sponsored links'. You must be wondering why this type of advertising is called pay per click? The beauty of PPC is that you only have to pay if a prospect clicks on your ad. Anyone clicking on your ad will be taken directly to your website. This is the major difference between ad placements in traditional media in which you have to pay whether you find buyers through them or not. There is another advantage in PPC advertising. This is a huge opportunity to monitor your traffic and understand your customer. You can chop and change your online PPC ads as you wish – even hourly.

Online Public relations

The objective of online PR is the same as traditional PR – to build reputation. Fortunately online PR takes less effort and money to execute because of the interconnectivity of websites. As a result you can insert favorable mention about your website on other related websites to create a good opinion and drive traffic to it. Online PR also serves another objective. You can create suitable backlinks to your website which will help you in getting higher search ranking. Reputation management is extremely important in managing your marketing effort. As already mentioned elsewhere, the modern buyer is knowledgeable and wants to know more about you. A favorable mention on other websites can go a long way in alleviating the anxiety of your prospective buyer. You can buy a spot in popular PR sites which can spread the good word about you.

Chapter 3 - Understanding the consumer mindset for writing mind-blowing copy

Customer is king. The entire purpose of internet marketing is to locate, attract and compel customers to but your product or service. The nature of marketing does not change whether you are into traditional markets or selling online. Understanding the customer is your primary and most important need. Who is your target customer? What does he or she want from you? What do they look like or what is their behavior like? These are questions which must be satisfactorily answered if you wish to succeed in internet marketing.

Is your customer profile is pretty well dispersed and spread over the demography or are they concentrated in one specific area. If you take the example of software professionals as a category of customers you will find them confined to the Bay area in California. Finance professionals tend to flock around New York. If you are selling dark suits and striped ties, you would be wasting your time targeting San Francisco since the software guys seldom wear anything but shorts and a smelly T-shirt(or not so smelly but crumpled shirt). If you are looking for customers around the globe you should ensure that you are not trying to sell a refrigerator to an Eskimo. You would be surprised to know how limited is your understanding of an international customer.

You can segment your customers under the category of age, sex, profession, social status and buying power. It is easier to target urban population compared to a dispersed rural buyer. The issues connected with transportation and delivery play an important part since the final cost or landed cost is dependent on these factors.

Purring customers into a straightjacketed stereotype is a mistake which you should avoid. The internet is no longer a place for the rich. You must also not assume that females prefer online purchases more than their counterparts. You will find teenagers going on binge buying while retirees and pensioners flock to websites because of the convenience factor. The motivations for different groups vary and can be mindboggling. Identifying your target group becomes critical under these circumstances.

From where do your customers access the internet for making purchases? You would assume that home would be the preferred location, but you could be mistaken. It has been discovered that men access adult sites from their offices. You would think that filters, firewalls and programs would be installed in offices to discourage such behavior, but surprisingly employees find novel ways to bypass such annoying impediments. This goes to show that customers will go out of the way to consume goods and services which they badly desire. It's your duty and obligation to find these people and respond suitably to their need.

This does not mean that you only have to look for desperados wanting adult gratification. You can find customers who will readily consume whatever you have to offer as long as you package it attractively.

Reading the mind of your customer

You don't have to be a diviner or a psychic to know what kind of customer will get attracted to your product or service. There are many ways to segment your customer according to their motivation.

The first kind of buyer is the one who is easy to please. You don't have to do much to convince such buyers because they are already pumped up for making a purchase. These buyers (whom you would classify as darlings) only want to know if you have the right product they are looking for. Providing detailed information is enough to make them take out their wallet. They are not overly price conscious and are likely to go for unknown brands without hesitation. It is obvious that these buyers would generally be found buying products which are not expensive.

The second kind is the buyers looking for Gucci, Louis Vuitton or exclusive shoes from Salvatore Ferragamo. These buyers may be hunting for bargains but they know their brands and their value. They cannot be fooled to buy duplicates or replicas. They buy online because of the convenience and they are secure in their knowledge that big names would not cheat them for the sake of a few dollars. They make costly and big purchases. Go for them if you are selling exclusive stuff but remember that they are extremely difficult to please.

You will also find buyers who are bargain hunters who go online for the thrill and fun. They may not spend much but they are indiscriminate. They will buy a Gucci lookalike knowing fully well that they are buying a fake. Labels don't matter to them. This segment can be an attractive one to target. You can offer bargains and discounts and they will fall for it.

The toughest group of buyers is the one who likes to feel and touch the products they buy.

There is no way you can offer this pleasure to them over the internet. Moreover they want bargains and discounts on top of their desire to ensure quality.

Lastly there is a vast contingent of people who are just window shipping. They like to browse stuff on the internet and find vicarious pleasure in their online outings. They may buy a product sometime in the unknown future but you should not bet on it.

Web browsing history

Website users stroll around like they usually do in a brick and mortar shopping mall. The pattern which they follow tells a tale about their shopping habits and buying history. Traditionally, window displays are designed to cater to the visitor's needs. Lesser bought items are necessarily stored in the back and only those products in demand are prominently displayed.

Internet marketers should employ the same tactics while soliciting customers online.

Building specific scenarios can not only foster better relationships but also make locating of products easier. Having segments dedicated to men, women and children is a time tested scenario which must be replicated. An additional advantage of a website compared to a traditional market is the ability to divert the visitor using links and navigation buttons. It has been observed that people tend to follow visual cues like use of big and bright colored buttons while browsing. This is the reason why you will find the 'buy' button prominently displayed on all webpages.

Understanding the consumer means winning half the battle. You should put aside a portion of your budget for researching the consumer before attempting to create your website.

Chapter 4 - Copywriting – from essential to critical to vital

Internet marketing has revolutionized buying. You can no longer feely or try out your jeans before buying. There are no changing rooms or trial rooms online. What you have is words to understand and appreciate whatever you want to buy. Words therefore have become vital to any online transaction. Copywriting skills are critical to your internet marketing effort. What goes into making a good copy? Here are some tips on converting good copy into copy which sells.

From machine language to being human

Digital does not mean speaking in machine language. Buyers are still human and they want to read legible words which are meaningful. This means you must speak to the buyer in terms of his needs and wants – not merely offer discount coupons. Effective copywriting should convince the reader about the elements which appeal emotionally to him or her. Keep an open mind while writing. By all means, become a robot if you are addressing an intellectual gathering (which presumably is your target audience). Your writing should be informal when you are speaking to the general public. Remember that informal does not mean casual. You should never write casually. Your tone should always be professional even when you are humorous.

Keep it simple not clever

This is a pitfall which all copywriters must avoid. It's very easy to seem clever and smart, but the customer reading your message is not going to like it. Don't make your customer feel inferior or stupid. Your consumers are kings and queens you must treat them like one. You must take this advice seriously because this mistake of treating customers like fools can be your last one. You can be clever among your peers. You can show your humor to people who are your equal but not to your prospects. The approach must always be respectful. Your customers know what is best for them. You only have to explain what you have to offer and how you will benefit them. Actually this attitude is not that difficult to follow.

What is simplicity in copywriting?

'Keep it simple'. 'Don't oversell'. 'Stick to the basics'. By now you must have got fed up of hearing this kind of advice and wondering want it actually means. On top of it, no one explains simplicity and basics which leads to further frustration.

These pearls of wisdom (can you detect the sarcasm?) originate from basic marketing principles. The first principle is not to oversell by behaving like a smartass. No one likes a smartass. You must stop thinking that you know everything. You don't. Your customers know more about what they want than you do. Do not teach. Do not be preachy. Don't give lectures. In the internet world, your customer has access to all kinds of information. People use Google often. They research the subject in which they are interested. Your customers are better informed than they were ten years back.

Simplicity here , in the context of copywriting, means informing your prospects about your offer, highlighting the advantages when compared to your competitor, showing the benefits in the form of good references and projecting a positive impression. You should do all this using simple language. Earlier (before the internet era), only big brands with deep pockets could survive. You are lucky to be living now. There are many ways to create a positive image about your product without busting a bank.

Chopping down the message to bare essentials

How do you sharpen a pencil? You first chop or whittle down the wood till the lead is visible. You don't start writing with a blunt lead, do you? You further sharpen the lead before you write. Copywriting works on the same principles. You first write a draft which contains the product description. This is the starting point. At this time you have the rough content. You now look at the value proposition. What are you offering to the customer in terms of benefits? Keep the value part of the proposition and chop off the rest. The lead of your content is now exposed, but the message is not yet ready. You have to remove words which are unnecessary. Barebones- basics-essentials. That's it. Let's look at an example.

The giraffe

'Our giraffe has a long neck and stands on four feet. With its long neck it can reach the highest branches of a tree and pluck the leaves with its mouth. Our giraffe also has spotted skin which is excellent for camouflage. Overall, our giraffe is an excellent buy and reasonably priced.'

Look at the message above. You will agree that all the features of a giraffe have been mentioned. For this very reason the message is unclear.

What will a customer do with the giraffe with so many features?

The chopped down giraffe

Are you looking for a giraffe which can reach up to fifteen feet and eat leaves on the upper branches of a tree?

Your customers may now look at this message of a chopped down giraffe and instantly connect with it. You have brought out a single benefit of a giraffe and highlighted it. Can you do more with the message?

The message

Buy now - Giraffe which can eat leaves from fifteen feet high branches.

Did you notice how the redundant words have been chopped off? This message appeals directly to those customers who are looking for this feature. It doesn't matter at all that most of the readers will ignore the message. What matters is that you have connected with the people who are looking for this specific feature. You are now speaking directly to your target audience. Still, there is one element missing. Why should someone buy your giraffe now if they can buy it anytime next week? There is no sense of urgency. Though there is a 'call to action', there seems to be no hurry.

Hurry. Limited stock. Buy giraffe now. Reach over 15 feet.

Or

Hurry. Massive discount on giraffe with 15 feet reach. Sale ends tomorrow.

What do you think of this message? You have introduced a sense of urgency now. Buyers are likely to make a purchase soon. Also notice that a buyer wanting to buy a giraffe already knows about them. You don't have to waste their time introducing them to the animal. You have cut the message and made it sharp. You have also created a sense of urgency. You have given the facts and now you only have to wait and receive the cash.

By the way, why mention a giraffe?

This chopping and trimming process is suitable for all your messages – Google AdWords, emails, blog posts, social media and even ebooks.

Using the above technique let's now look at how you may write an online article, email or any content for that matter. You must keep the flow of ideas and concepts in mind while going through the steps.

Start with the end in mind

It's like writing a suspense novel. You already know the end even before you start writing the first word.

Use your imagination

Imagination and creative writing go together. Imagine what the guy reading your message looks like? Give wings to your imagination. Let your thoughts go wild (not in the way you are now thinking). Get into the mind of your customer. Is this person young or old? Rich or poor? How does this person spend his evening? What really excites him? Is this person likely to read your email or directly put it in trash? Create a mental picture and try to sell him your product.

In short, put yourself in your customer's shoes and observe where it pinches. Remove the bit where it pinches and offer the shoe for sale. Pitch your message at the right audience. Explain the benefits. Throw some juicy discounts. Give a warning – now or never. And win the order.

Think of benefits not features

It's good to know that you have a good product. It is certainly useful. But don't be carried away by the features of your product. Your customer is not really interested in your life saving drug. He simply wants a solution for the itch on his back (the place he can't reach). If you can offer a product for curing itches, you are through.

How are you better than your competitor?

This is extremely important. There will be many people selling products which have a need. Popular solutions have high demand and the competition is fierce. You must differentiate yourself from your competitor. Remember not to offer incremental benefits. This won't work. You must offer dramatically different or massively improved product. This differentiation must be visible even to the blind – it must be obvious. Copywriting skills should focus on differentiators.

The height of differentiation is making a USP (Unique selling proposition). Focus on one benefit and make it unique. No one else in the market offers this specific benefit. There is no visible competition. You can create a USP in different ways. Amazon started by selling books over the internet. The product (book) was the same but the delivery process was unique. It was convenient. The books were delivered home. What a great benefit for busy people. They no longer had to visit bookshops to buy their favorite novel. Amazon now sells over $5 billion worth of books online annually. Absolutely amazing isn't it?

The USP message

You may have a great USP but does your writing send that message? In online or internet marketing, the headline is king. Readers seldom go beyond reading the heading and skip to another web page if they find you dull or boring. You must get your headline right and to the point. If you are sending an e-mail make sure that the headline compels recipients to open the mail. You need attention grabbing headlines. Remember not to make claims you can't follow through. Make use of adjectives. Sprinkle your message liberally with great words. Communicate enthusiasm and energy. End your message with a call to action. Give them a carrot.

Converting prospects into customers

In the end what matters is the sale. Your job, as an internet marketer, is to take people from the point of enquiry to a confirmed buyer. In the sales process, it is fairly easy to get people to the water but is difficult to make them drink. Prospects behave like horses in a race. They are finicky, fussy and choosy when they are asked to press the buy button. This is a universal experience. Car salesmen will vouch for this consumer behavior. Customers in a car showroom will nod their head appreciatively and make the right noises right up to the moment when they have to take a call. At this very moment, the almost convinced prospect, whom you had led along faithfully till now tries to flee the showroom. And do you know what the experienced salesmen do? Throw a free seat cushion as an incentive. And it works. Would you believe it? People are convinced to buy a car costing a few thousand dollars because they are offered an incentive worth a few dollars. This is human psychology.

The most important part of a sales process is call to action. How do you get people to tip over from prospects to buyers?

In internet marketing you are far removed physically from your customer. You only have the written word to convince the buyers. You better have great writing skills to succeed online. Call to action does not mean begging the prospect to buy. This strategy does not work. Your words should be powerful and empowering. Guiding your visitor through the buying process is important. People often abandon sites because there is no clear buying process. Build urgency in your copy. Offer discounts which have a clear end date.

Always give a sweet little discount or incentive when the visitor reaches the end of buying process. There are software's which use artificial intelligence to track the actions of visitors and offer appropriate discounts. Have you noticed how airlines offer discounts? The fare keeps changing depending on your actions.

In this chapter you have learnt about all the trick of copywriting trade. Now is the time to go ahead and implement it.

Chapter 5 - Tricks in writing a great sales page which will sell your product like hot cakes

Assuming that you have already done your bit by enticing prospects to your website, what steps are you taking to convert them into customers? You would be surprised to know that many internet marketers spend an enormous amount of time, resources and money to bring people to their doorsteps and then suddenly leave them to find their way. A great online promotion must be accompanied by a greater sales page. The sales page, if done properly, can lead to higher conversions.

Your online ad strategy must seamlessly merge with your offering. This means that you must fulfil promises which you have made while inviting customers to have a look at your product or service. There are many outcomes which you be looking for other than selling. You may like visitors to your website to simply complete a survey or watch a demo of your product, but once they enter your website, they must be compelled to convert into buyers.

There is no way to develop a landing page or sales page. Everything depends on your product or service, your target audience and your overall marketing strategy. You should keep your landing page simple yet focused with an eye on selling process.

Tips for Creating Effective Landing Page Which Converts Like Crazy

In the end, your product is only as good as your copy. Fantastic products fail because they are not marketed properly and poor products sell like crazy because of the copy. Your sales page must be able to enthuse, energize and galvanize your would-be customers. What you write is the key to success. Never underestimate the power of your message – sometimes the message itself sells regardless of the product. Make sure that your landing page has all the elements which a customer would be looking for.

The first paragraph of your landing page should explicitly mention what is on offer. Don't dilly-dally. Don't put if's and but's. Explain in a simple language. Your landing page should take off from what you have mentioned in your online advertisement. You must elaborate and expand on your initial offer. You must carry your visitor from mere interest to a desire to buy. The landing page must ensure conversion. Give information which is essential. If you are selling a refrigerator, talk about its benefits and how it compares with your competitors. Highlight your advantages. Explore the good points. Explain the value proposition. Focus on the joy and pleasure which a customer would derive by purchasing your product.

Many sales people get carried away by the features of their product. For example, salesmen could highlight the purity of the coffee they sell. Have you stopped for a moment and thought why a customer would get excited by purity of coffee? Instead, what if you tell your customers that your coffee tastes like heaven and will transport them into a world of bliss? You get the point? You must focus on benefits and not on the features of your product. Basically what you are doing is answering the most important question – What is in it for me?

Sometimes marketers, in their enthusiasm or greed, tend to exaggerate the benefits of products in their initial offering. In other words, they fail to deliver what they had promised. Never assume that your customer is a fool. You will be fooling yourself if you do so. Promise only what you deliver and you can will find customers. Don't disappoint your customers or you will face the consequences. There is always something which your product does better than a competitor's. Highlight these benefits. Add color to the roses by all means, but don't sell apples when you promise them oranges.

You should not bundle all customers in one basket. Putting them in a sack and treating customers like potatoes or onions is a mistake.

Your customer is human with emotions, sensitivities, likes and dislikes. Treat them like human beings. Be considerate. Treat them with respect when they visit your website. An important consideration, which you must keep in mind, is the fact that not everyone is alike. Think about your target audience and create your sales page keeping this market in mind. You can't cater to everyone. Now, create a seamless experience, right from the online ad to the sale of your product. People who buy diamonds don't buy shoe lace. Imagine that you are selling a diamond ring to an about-to-become bridegroom. Now imagine you are selling commonplace shoes. Do you think the sales process should be the same? Not that you have to treat the shoe buyer with disdain. You have to treat them differently. This customer is looking for comfort, ease of use and economy, but they will eventually pay for the shoes just as the buyer of diamonds. They are both important customers – only they are different with different needs.

Online or internet marketing is nuanced. It caters to the modern customer who is impatient and always in a hurry. You have to catch their attention within a fraction of a second or you are likely to lose them. The heading or caption must be enticing and immediately draw attention. That's why so much emphasis is put on great captions and headlines. You must spend time to tweak your headlines and watch the reaction of your target audience. You should fine tune your pitch to perfection. Compel your customer to click on your online advertisement and follow through with your promise.

Your impatient, pampered, spoilt and slippery customers no longer want to read pages of creative writing. They want short and to-the-point messages which convey the facts. Moreover, it's difficult to read large amount of text on screen and smartphones. Keeping messages short and sweet should do the trick. Of course, you should avoid convoluted jargon which can obfuscate and befuddle customers.

Rather you should use simple words which people can read and understand easily.

Do you realize that your going-to-be customer is taking a hug risk by buying from you? He is totally dependent on your word. He can neither see nor feel the product he is buying. Not like a shop where a customer can actually see the stuff he wants to buy. Naturally, your online customer is likely to behave like a horse on the racecourse – finicky and fussy. What should you do to put this man at ease? Probably a money-back guarantee should do the trick. The customer knows that he can claim a refund if he does not like the product. Money-back policy seems to be risky for sellers but you should know that very few customers tend to avail this offer.

Buyers like free gifts, discounts and freebies. Why not give them what they want? Maybe you can offer them free shipping? A freebie which costs you almost nothing but will keep your customer in good spirits? Reward points for future purchase can also make your customer smile.

Have you noticed that many visitors to your website simply vanish when it comes to clicking the buy button? This last minute panic is natural and should be managed by you. You must create a sense of urgency – probably the offer which is quite attractive will last for only two hours. Maybe the product is selling like hot cakes and will be out of stock ......in a few minutes!!

An online customer is pampered. He has many options and offers. If you don't create a sense of urgency, you will lose him for sure. You must convey that your offer is not only the best but will also expire quickly. You may think that customers are smart and understand these sales gimmicks – they do. But at the same time they also fall for it every time.

When a customer walks into a shop, he can touch, feel, try and experience the products he wants to buy. Online, he is flying blind. You should ensure that this online customer can find a way to authenticate your site. Testimonials are an excellent way to convince customers. Getting a reputed rating agency to evaluate you is a nice way to put your customer at ease. It's all about credibility. Are you what you claim to be? Will you keep your word or steal from your customer's credit card?

The biggest issue in online marketing is to make a customer provide his credit card details. The internet is filled with horror stories about fakes and swindlers who steal credit card details and rob foolish customers. You need trustworthiness and credibility if you want customers to share their credit card details.

You should not shy away from selling. Providing a 'buy' or 'register' button makes good sense. Don't make your customer to search for the buy button - lead him to it.

Tips for Planning the Layout of Your Landing Page

Now that you know more about landing pages it's time to move ahead and design one. Keep the following in mind and you never fail in your objective – to convert visitors into customers.

Did you notice that you read the material above the fold and decide whether to scroll down a web page? The visitor to your landing page may as well abandon your site if he finds nothing exciting at first glance. It therefore makes sense to put your best foot forward right at the place where it is most likely to be noticed. Get the adrenaline of your visitor flowing right way by giving him the material when he needs it. You must avoid the very top of your landing page to showcase your product. Why should you avoid the best place where your content is most likely to be read? You will notice that this place is usually reserved for banner ads. Readers tend to skip the top part of a web page accustomed to the fact that it contains ads.

You must keep the visitor on-page by letting your content flow from one topic to another.

Excessive white spaces and line breaks give the impression that the reader has reached the end of the page.

Make sure that your tone and color schemes are carried forward from your online ads and newsletters to your landing page. Make it a seamless experience. Let the customer get used to your color schemes and page payout. Keep the goal in mind always. Don't let the visitors click on an external link and walk away from your site. Closing the sale is an art which you should master. Create urgency as you go from one step to another. Behave as if there is no tomorrow. This is a tough act but sales require such kind of focus.

Give your visitor lots of opportunity to ask more questions. Better still; give them a chance to view more options. Provide them with information on security, shipping, return policy and exchange issues. Answer all questions with FAQ section.

A single picture is worth a thousand words. Including images and graphics to entice the visitor is certainly a good idea. Use pleasant colors schemes and fonts to attract and impress customers.

Though your customer may have moved online, the psychology still remains the same. People want to talk to someone who is not a machine before making a final decision. Why not give them a phone number to call and speak to another fellow human? A pleasant voice on the other end of the phone line can push a visitor to go for it. Give your customers a chance to make a purchase – not a reason to escape from your website.

Remember that your website is for business purposes and not for charity (unless it is for charity). Visitors know that they are being solicited. You may want visitors to fill a form which might look like a fairly simple deal. But wait! People don't like to share personal information unless there is an incentive to do so. Even getting a simple form filled by visitors may become a challenge. You have to give something in return to the visitor. A free ebook on related subject may turn the tide in your favor. You can even promise to give a discount coupon when visitors provide information.

You should not ask too many questions. Don't copy-paste a questionnaire from somewhere else. Many questions may not be relevant to you. Your purchase process must lead the buyer through a clear and meaningful manner. All questionnaires must be relevant and to the point. Don't ask questions which are not pertinent and on a subject under discussion. Don't give a buyer any opportunity to abandon the buying process. Don't ask for their phone number right in the middle of making a sale. It doesn't matter to you now. Studies have shown that every small increment in number of questions proportionally decreases your chances of selling.

As far as the design of your landing page is concerned , it should load fast, be compatible with all popular browsers like Internet Explorer, Google Chrome and Mozilla Firefox, be simple and, attractive to use. Many websites don't work on all browsers or don't work properly which may lead to loss of business.

The nuts and bolts of a landing page

You have no option but to create the perfect sales page. What this mean is that you have to tailor the message according to your product. Each landing page is unique and specific to your product.

Every aspect of your landing page depends on your product. If you are selling an industrial product you have to explain the benefits. Don't cram everything in one page. This looks daunting and the reader may not be able to get the information which they want. Breakdown your content into several pages. The main page, which is the landing page, should provide the big picture – what, how and why. Nothing else. Provide links to the pages which contain the details. Readers who want to know more will click on these links and get the information they need. This approach will lead to better conversions. Make sure that the links do not take the visitor away to another website. This will be a disaster. Keep visitors on the same website, pushing them to buy immediately.

Focus should remain on one single product. A landing page is not appropriate for all products. If you are into retail segment, you are better off with a website featuring all your products. Here too, you must allow the visitors to navigate on their own and arrive at the purchase page.

Paying attention to your target audience is important. What language do they speak? Don't teach Mandarin to the Japanese. People speak in languages other than English. Cultures and local customs are factors which impact on the purchase process. Did you know that the Chinese love to bargain? You must understand the international market if you wish to be successful at selling worldwide.

Internet users have been pampered and don't like to type information. Give them auto-filled order forms in which the name, address and other simple details are already filled in. Reduce the workload of the buyer as far as possible. Let the buyer click on the buy button and be done with it.

There are many business intelligence tools which assist you in pulling visitors to the landing page. CRM packages have literally become smart and business savvy. You can consider intelligence tools if you have the budget for them.

Online marketing too is based on the same principles as traditional marketing. Repeat customers are cheaper and more accessible. You should not abandon your customer after he or she makes a purchase. Think of the life-time value of this customer. You must follow-up on the current purchase. Make attractive offers and provide discounts to loyal customers. Loyalty programs are popular because they are based on established psychological principles.

You must steer your customers with all the psychological tools available to you. Manage the expectations and you can manage your customers. Compel your customer to buy and buy now. Don't let them escape because of any perceived deficiency like trust and faith in your ability to deliver. Take all steps necessary to develop a sense of trust.

You must monitor and track the progress of visitors to the landing page. Why do they abandon your site? Which factors may be affecting their decision? It all boils down to one simple question - What do the customers really want? If you can determine this, you are a winner.

Chapter 6 - Swipe files and how to do it the right way

Have you ever taken a swipe at anybody? No, you are not going to learn about kicking someone's face in. You will not learn about that kind of swipe in this chapter. The 'swipe file' we are talking about is going to help you get up from your sleep and start writing great copy. Internet marketing is incomplete without understanding the mind of consumers and feeding them material which they want. You must have, by now, read some great copy and wondered when you will be able to write as well. Sigh! This is not going to happen if you keep reading in the hope that one day you will start writing the same way.

The trick is to keep reading but differently. Ah, does this mean reading while wearing dark glasses? Not funny. The idea is to read what is being written from marketing point of view. Why do some websites, emails, blog posts and articles create an impact? How do copywriters convince their customers to buy stuff which they don't really care about? Is there a method to the madness?

Swiping in this context means taking someone else's content and rewriting in your own words. Isn't it plagiarizing? Won't you get penalized for it by Google? Or worse, get dragged to court for committing a criminal offence.

Swiping is not plagiarizing. In fact swiping is creative work. Famous artists and painters have confessed that they have been inspired by other cultures and arts. What they actually mean is that they have copied others. But do we say that about them? Swiping is creating something new or novel y taking the best from others.

The process of swiping

All of us read articles, blog posts and emails which suddenly causes us to sit up and take notice. The writing feels so inspiring, original and creative that you wish you had written it. But we simply let it go and forget about it. If you are a writer, there would have been many occasions when you felt in need of motivation. What if you had created a swipe file containing all the great copy you had read and inspired by? You could have immediately referred to it and come up with your own Nobel Prize winning copy. So, next time you read something inspirational, just jot it down in your swipe file. You can bookmark the web page for future reference. You can have a swipe file made of bookmarks. Do you know how to create folders in bookmarks? If not, you must begin today. Bookmark your favorites in appropriate folders – copywriting, suspense novels, swimming, cooking recipes etc.

Most of us face problems in kicking-off projects. Your creative engine takes years to warm up and by this time your client is fuming and billowing smoke from his backside. Not a pleasant sight or a feeling. The swipe file helps you to kick start your writing projects. You can quickly look up the swipe file and start writing. The process becomes easy because you have simply copied the idea from someone else. Did you notice that you have copied the idea, concept and flow – not the actual words? If you stop and think for a few minutes, it's the idea which counts. Modern word processors, like Microsoft Word let you get hold of synonyms with just a click of your mouse. You must not copy the style of a famous copywriter. You must observe, learn and create your own style of writing. A swipe file should be used to make a template. You can use the swipe file for inspiration, formatting styles, structure and writing great headlines.

For the purpose of internet marketing, a swipe file should be analyzed from the following viewpoint –

1. You must study and analyze web pages from the standpoint of their value they impart to the overall impact. Home pages have a particular design. They urge or compel you to explore further. They are sometimes teasers which make you click on other links. The about page has a different structure. They tell you about the people who are behind the product or service

which is being sold. It creates gravity, authenticity and makes the website legitimate and dependable. The sales page brings to the reader the immediacy, urgency and desire to buy now. Each page has its own story to sell (tell).

2. Each web page must be seen with a magnifying lens. What is the purpose or raison d'etre of that page? Is it able to convey the message clearly and without ambiguity? What action is the reader inspired to take? Does the page content lead the reader from point A to B effortlessly? Does the page have flow or is does it look disjointed?

3. How is a web page different from an email or a blog post? This is the most important aspect you should study. Amateurs believe that content writing is the same for a web page, blog post or an email. This assumption must be swiped from your mind and firmly replaced with the fact that writing from different platforms is different because the end goal is different. You may want readers to click on a link if you are sending

emails. You may want people to register for your newsletter if you are writing a blog post. Your landing page is the culmination of your efforts. This is the do-or-die page. Readers have to be converted right here on this very landing page. You have to put your heart into creating this page. Your swipe file should have over twenty examples of a landing page. In fact, it's absolutely amazing to analyze landing pages designed by expert copywriters. These pages effortlessly take the reader through the purchase process. You must thoroughly break these masterpieces into smaller bits and analyze them with a microscope.

A swipe file is an essential part of a copywriter's toolkit. You can create impactful and highly effective content using swipe files. Swiping is not plagiarism because you are not copying the actual words but only the idea and concept. Learn about the structure, flow and control from masters of this art and do what has already been done – but differently.

Chapter 7 - The sales funnel

The most important concept in internet marketing is the sales funnel. The process is exactly the same as an actual funnel – you have lots of prospects at the top and they get filtered out as they go down the funnel. In the end you get genuine customers who pay for your product or service. Designing a sales funnel is an art as well as a science. Psychologists have dug deep into the minds of customers and have created the concept of a sales funnel. Here you will learn about the ingredients and how to design an effective sales funnel.

As an entrepreneur, you understand marketing's importance: Without marketing, your business would eventually fail due to the absence of new customers. Therefore, if you haven't already put time and effort into this mission, now is the time to start; and one easy way to start is the utilization of a sales funnel.

Let your customers land softly on your website

There is a tendency to force would-be customers to make a purchase immediately as soon as they land on a website. Customers, on the other hand, don't like to be forced. In the end you lose visitors who could have been your customers. Let people land smoothly on your website. Give them an opportunity to explore. Entice them, cajole them and convince them. To do this successfully you must have great content. By this we do not mean great English. In fact the simpler you keep things better it is for you. Don't even hint that you are planning to sell anything to them. This is the first step in the sales funnel.

First impression counts when it concerns your website. Give your visitors something to chew on. Prepare them for the next step.

The second step is to expose the visitor to your product or service. Give them a good reason to consider you. What are you offering? How is it better than any competitor's offer? What incentive are you giving for making a purchase now? The purpose is to create a desire, a need, a craving to buy from you. Remember that more acute the craving, more the opportunity to make a sale. Notice that you are not jumping on the back of the visitor and pounding his head with your offer. This guy is still exploring; still trying to make up his mind. This is pre-sell at its best. What happens if the prospect decides to abandon the site at this moment? You can hang on to a reluctant prospect. No amount of hard sell will be able to keep him onsite. Kicking up a storm will only be counterproductive. The initial stage of the stage funnel should only whet the appetite of the would-be buyer.

The third stage of the sales funnel is crucial to success. The prospect is primed. He is mentally ready to buy. Something is holding him from pressing the buy button. What is it? You must provide an incentive to the visitor to but your product now. You can offer an attractive discount or a free gift which would be impossible to ignore. Put a time stamp on your offer. Make the visitor believe that he or she would miss a fantastic opportunity if he doesn't buy now.

There are two equally likely outcomes of this strategy. The buyer decides to go for it and takes the necessary steps to make a purchase. This is the best time to make him buy a costlier item because it is more attractive. You must try to upsell at this moment.

The other outcome is that the prospect may not be convinced and decides to quit your site. Once again, don't let the prospect leave. Don't give up at this stage. You still have an opportunity to make a sale. This is the time to down sell. Provide option to buy a lower priced item. Prospects with smaller budgets may opt for your cheaper products.

You are wrong if you think that you have reached the end of sales funnel by converting prospects into buyers. Nurturing your customers is more important than making a single sale. Offer exclusive deals, membership cards, free newsletters and other incentives to keep them coming again and again. Squeeze every small drop from your effort.

Sales funnel revisited

So, here is the problem – you want as many prospects or would-be buyers into your net which is called the sales funnel. Many kinds of people qualify as prospects, maybe millions of them. How do you get in touch with all of them? How do you tell them that you exist? And do you really need such a huge net? You need to filter out and condense your target audience even before they get into the sales funnel, right? Lead generation should be approached from a dispersed mindset. Look at what you already have. Do you have an effective search engine system in place? Good, that's a beginning. Can you afford a Google paid ad campaign? Great, add this in your basket of to-do list. You have a Facebook account, a blog or access to an online magazine. All these channels are part of your sales funnel. Don't start sweating out the details. You must wait and watch the target trickling in. Provide more information to people who ask. Provide information anyway. At this moment, don't shove your product or service down their throat. People don't like getting shoved one bit. You are just getting acquainted with the clients - getting to know them sort of.

Now these leads are getting interested and want to know more. They are into the sales funnel. Feed them with more information. Give them more details. Slowly introduce your product. Let them know why your product suits them. Highlight the positives. Don't oversell. Don't force. Keep educating and have patience.

Once your leads are halfway through your sales funnel, you can get into specifics. At this time you should be ready for your carefully nurtured lead to abandon you. This may happen due to many reasons. Your leads need an incentive and some gentle persuasion to take the next step.

Maybe its holiday time and your discount offer will end soon. You can add a freebie to egg your leads on.

Note that everything need not happen within the confines of your website. Email newsletters are a great way to keep your leads interested. Your emails must be customized and speak to individual customers. People hate to be clubbed over their head and attacked by spammy emails.

Keep your leads engaged till they reach the bottom of your sales funnel. Your effort should be to convert leads and prospects into customers, once you reach the final closing stages. Closing sales is an art and deserves a whole book for a detailed explanation. Learn to close sales. Remember the last time you bought a car which you didn't really want? The salesman in that showroom knew how to close sales. At the same time you need not be sleazy and crooked to convert customers. For long term customer loyalty you must first be moral and right.

In the end, you should remember that a sales funnel is only as good as your internet marketing strategy. Don't get stuck with three step or five step sales funnel. Be creative and look at the big picture. There can be an overlap in the steps or you can quicken the pace of conversation. Everything depends on the situation.

Chapter 8 - Affiliate programs

The problem: You don't have a product to sell.

The solution: You don't need a product to sell.

Neat. Tidy. Simple. This is called affiliate marketing.

If you have been reading this ebook on internet marketing and wondered if you will ever be able to use all the techniques, here is the perfect solution – Affiliate programs. In this kind of selling you don't need a cent – well, you don't need loads of cash. You don't need a product. The only thing you need is enthusiasm and belief that you can be a great affiliate.

What is an affiliate program?

In simple terms, affiliate program is selling someone else's product. Why not call yourself a reseller instead? There is a huge difference between an affiliate and a reseller.

As a reseller, you have to first buy from the producer, keep it in stock, advertise, and ship the product. What this means is that you need lots of money to become a reseller. The advantage of reselling is that you get to keep the profits from the sale. As an affiliate you can do away with all the burden of a reseller and yet earn handsomely. One question which may arise in your mind is this: If becoming an affiliate is more beneficial than reselling, why has it become popular only now? The main reason is the setting up an affiliate business. Internet technology has facilitated automation of many functions and this is the reason why affiliate programs have become popular.

The benefits of an affiliate program

Another question which may popup in your mind is why everyone has not joined the affiliate bandwagon if it is so insanely popular. The reason is simple – people do not know internet marketing. This is where you take a lead. You already know the tricks of the trade and can easily market a product online. This is the only requirement to become a successful affiliate.

Another reason why not everyone makes the grade is because people begin with misconceptions, that they can sit back and the money will just keep piling up in their bank account automatically. Though you don't have to spend huge amount of money, you still have to put in effort and your time into the process.

Warning: You have to be serious and committed if you want to succeed in this line of business. Don't expect to experience joy without putting in hard work.

In affiliate marketing there is a problem of plenty. There are thousands of products which are doing well and it becomes difficult to decide what to sell and what to avoid. The only piece of advice is to select a niche and stick to it. Maybe you are good in writing which means you can naturally good at selling books. Sportspersons can choose to sell sports goods, musicians can sell music..............

If you are such a good internet marketer, why not sell your own product? Consider this: as a producer and seller you can sell one product or at best two. As an affiliate you can sell hundreds of products. You will never be stuck with a product. Your business will never suffer a loss because you don't own anything. You can pick and choose. You can stop marketing a product anytime you want.

As a primary seller, you require employees to make the product- design and manufacture. You have to pay their salaries regardless of whether you sell your product or not. You have fixed costs like machinery. You have to pay regular rent. Why bother when there is a ready product for you to sell.

You don't even have to pay for joining an affiliate program (be careful if someone asks you to pay to join as an affiliate). You don't have to show your degree to become an affiliate. Your background does not matter. You can make a clean break from your existing job and start afresh as an affiliate. You don't need special knowledge or sales background.

As an affiliate you don't need to build your reputation. This is the hardest part in the sales process. Reputation building can take years and loads of money. As an affiliate you are ready to go. The hard work has been done for you.

People who have built their own online business know how difficult it is to create a payment gateway. Ask for the credit card details and the prospect will run away as if attacked by wild dogs. You don't have to be worried by the prospect of managing wild dogs. As an affiliate there aren't any. Managing a website, manufacturing a product, juggling the inventory and worrying about shipping and insurance are only a few issues which an affiliate does not have to bother about.

How does an affiliate program work?

There are many affiliate programs which you can join. You will learn about some popular affiliate programs in the next chapter. The process of joining an affiliate program is simple.

1.   First you must have a look at what is on offer. There are many affiliate programs and therefore you must be able to identify one which gives you maximum returns.

2.   Create a website to match the product you have chosen. Use all the tricks and advice provided in this book to create content which attracts buyers.

3.   What have you learnt about creating an effective sales page? Make use of the strategies to promote the product you want.

4.   Remember that you have already chosen the products which you want to sell. This is the time to join your chosen affiliate program. The advantage of beginning with the end in mind is that your site is ready to be assessed. Many affiliate programs give you membership only

after they have had a look at your website. Don't assume that you can fool them. Anyway, you won't make any money if you cannot attract buyers.

5. You can sign up for more than one affiliate program. You need to dedicate pages for specific products related to one affiliate program.

6. Don't sit back and wait for customers. You have to actively promote your site to attract good prospects.

7. Follow up with a good analytics program. Know what a visitor does on your website. Change content and design appropriately to increase your sales.

That's it. You are well on your way to becoming a Super Affiliate.

Chapter 9 - Highest paying affiliate programs

Affiliate marketing has changed the way we do business. It is one of the defining aspects of internet marketing. Imagine a salesperson on hormones! Imagine someone getting rich without investing much upfront! Imagine democratization of wealth! Affiliate marketing is all this and more. Affiliate marketing was introduced by none other than Amazon. It opened up opportunities for millions of people who could not afford to invest huge amount of money in business. It's obvious that Amazon should be your first stop if you want to win in this form of business activity. But before you start, remember that affiliate marketing may not require much of an investment in terms of cash but it does require effort. You have to undertake certain activities which are unavoidable.

As explained earlier, there are thousands of affiliate opportunities. People can and do get lost in the maze. The bestselling products need not be the best for you – due to different reasons. The competition may be too fierce and you may be the last entrant. The product which is popular may already have been juiced. The product may be too technical for you to understand and sell. So, how do you really choose a product?

Ideally, you should not pick one product but a basket of products. Think about wellness. Within wellness you can have many products. You can play with products with different prices – very low to insanely high. You can experiment and study the dynamics of payouts in terms of commission and volume of sales. You will find articles on the internet which will tell you that you must choose products with high price because you will get higher commission. What they don't tell you is that price and volume of sales are interrelated. Higher the price, lower the volume. A 4% commission on a product with high turnover can give you better returns than products with 10% commission with low sales. You would be extremely lucky to find a product with a pricy label and also high sales volume. Enjoy.

Before you dip your hands into the affiliate soup, you must understand some of the terminology. An affiliate network, like Amazon, is only a link between the publishers, who are the product owners and you who is called a merchant. Why do you need an in-between? Can't the seller or publisher directly link with the seller? You require an affiliate network because they provide many technical services which an individual seller cannot develop with spending an exorbitant amount of money. The affiliate network must be able to track purchases from seller platform, establish that the payment has been received by the publisher, calculate and send commission to the seller and manage the entire process from end to end.

You will gain by joining an affiliate network because you can easily locate some great products and access tracking and analytics tools which will give you a low down on all your activities. You get all these benefits free of cost. The merchants, however, may have to pay to join the network.

You, the seller, gets paid depending on the affiliate model. Cost-Per-Sale (CPS) means you will only earn if someone clicks on a link in your site and then buys the product from the affiliate site. You must provide a lead which culminates in a sale. This affiliate model is the most popular among the lot since you only get paid when the buyer makes a purchase and pays for the product.

Cost-Per-Action (CPA) is another affiliate model in which the seller gets paid depending on predetermined actions to be performed by the lead. Cost-per-click and cost-per-impression are two CPA models used by some affiliate programs.

Now that you know the basic structure of an affiliate program, here are the top five you can join.

Amazon Affiliate program

It is by far the most popular affiliate program. Joining is easy as a breeze. What you must ensure is that you have the product basket (explained earlier) worked out. You must create an effective website with the product basket in mind. Once you are done, you can go to the Amazon affiliate program for registration. You can create an account by filling in personal particular. You will have to add the address of your website. Don't forget to provide details of your bank account to which you will receive your commission. Click on the Amazon Associates agreement and you are done.

You may have to wait to get approval from Amazon after which you can add your affiliate products which you wish to sell. Go through the documentation which is extensive and get a feel of the affiliate program.

Now promote your product basket and enjoy.

Clickbank

Clickbank has been around for a very long time and is popular among digital product marketers. The products are priced much higher than Amazon and the commission is also therefore handsome. There are reports that choosing products in Clickbank is easier. There is another advantage to joining Clickbank affiliate network. The products sold through Clickbank are usually not found elsewhere. Digital books on wellness, health, self-help and spirituality are popular and are known to be bestsellers. You can create a website on a product category and start selling with techniques which you are already familiar with. Registration on Clickbank is fairly easy and similar to Amazon. The process is simple and you can follow instructions.

CJ Affiliate

Earlier known as commission Junction, this affiliate site is among the top five. This program has an extensive library of articles on affiliate marketing and is worth a read. It provides insight into some interesting aspects of selling online. CJ Affiliate has a fairly easy registration process. The affiliate program website can be viewed in five languages.

eBay affiliate program

This is another popular affiliate program which requires no introduction. The best part about eBay is that you can sell everyday use or daily use products which move fast. You may find that the price tag is of most products is pretty reasonable. Though the commission may be modest, you can make it up by selling high volumes. Registration is once again quite easy.

ReviMedia

Are you one of those who like to sell insurance and finance services? If yes, here is a great affiliate program specializing in this niche. The ReviMedia affiliate is easy to join and is focused on a specific niche. The platform provides excellent lead generation insights. A high percentage of lead on ReviMedia comes from mobile devices which is the preferred media today.

There are many affiliates that focus on specific niche which you can explore in addition to the above five affiliate programs. Overall, affiliate programs are excellent if you want to get into business in a short time.

Chapter 10 - Email marketing - getting close to the customer

Email marketing is a powerful tool to discover new prospects and to keep active customers engaged. Internet marketers must create suitable strategies to deploy this handy and useful tool to boost customer base and enable effective customer retention.

Both inbound and outbound email strategies are extremely useful for your business. Outbound email marketing means reaching out to prospective customers with your offerings and persuading them to purchase your products and services. It has been seen that internet marketers do not pay sufficient attention to inbound email marketing because they do not see value. This is an erroneous assumption. Customer retention is only possible when you respond in a timely and effective manner to customer feedback and complaints.

There are some issues which have recently emerged regarding email marketing. Spamming has become all pervasive to an extent that legislative measures have been put in place to tackle the menace. As a result email marketing has got a bad name and internet strategists have started recommending to their clients to avoid this mode of marketing. This extremely reaction seems like throwing the baby with the bathwater. There are legitimate ways through which you can still undertake an effective email campaign and benefit from it. Managing email lists of purely opt-in customers eliminate the issue of spam altogether. It has been seen that email marketing still drives good customer response as long as you respect their privacy and don't bombard them with your offerings. In fact email marketing is a vital cog in the overall internet marketing strategy of any company.

There are some key elements of email marketing which you must monitor carefully. You must monitor the delivery rate of your emails which will indicate whether you are able to reach out to the intended audience. Outdated and redundant email addresses can give you a false sense of achievement. Many customers have installed spam filters in their email applications which contain the menace of spams of which your email may become the unintended victim. You must know various techniques to avoid getting falsely identified as spam by the spam filters. Many web based email services have incorporated ways to authenticate emails to ensure that the sender of the email is genuine and is really the same as he claims to be.

Email marketing automation programs like Aweber and mailchimp allow you to create stunning email newsletters and also provide tool for monitoring the success rate.

You can monitor the 'open rate' of your emails which tells you which images in your html messages were clicked by the customer. However, you should be aware that email readers like Outlook Express block images automatically which mean that your feedback regarding clicks would not be accurate. You can monitor the 'clickrate' of your email messages to estimate the success of your email campaign.

Due to reasons mentioned earlier, you should ensure that the recipients of your emails are genuine leads and you are not spamming your would-be customers. You can acquire an effective email database using any of the following methods –

1. By renting an email list

This is by far the easiest and cheapest way to build your email list. It is also the least efficient. First of all you would be hard put to verify the genuineness of the list. As a thumb rule, the cheaper the email list more the chances are that it is useless. Renting email lists is popular with financial service providers because there is a general feeling that recipients would not mind receiving offers from them. However, renting email lists is still considered black hat. In the long run, cheap lists tend to have higher cost per acquisition or CPA.

2. Riding piggyback on another popular brand

This is called co-branding and is popular with traditional marketers. This strategy can be highly effective since your own brand would gain form an existing brand presence. There is one drawback – a strong brand should agree to co-brand with you.

3. Inserting ads in another e-newsletter

There exists an opportunity to insert paid ads in a third party e-newsletter. In this case your ad is as good as the reputation of the company creating and distributing the newsletter. You should be careful while choosing a partner for this kind of service. Customers would usually mark these e-newsletters as spam if too many ads are carried in a single newsletter.

It has been found that your own in-house email list generated through your website is the best way to solicit customers. You can provide suitable incentive for visitors to opt-in to your email or newsletters. You can follow up with emails announcing special discounts and new arrivals which may be useful for your prospects. There is also less chance of your email going into the spam folder.

Designing effective email newsletters

What should you include in your email newsletters to make them more effective? The first is looks. All said and done, an attractive email can turn on the charm like nothing else. Use bright but creative colors, suitable fonts and attractive images. Your email should be created for specific group of customers. It should be relevant and address the needs of people who will be the recipients. You should create a hook to attract customers. Give away freebies, generous discounts and seasonal gifts to attract buyers. Remember that acquiring a customer costs money and effort. Tailor made emails are more effective than one fit all.

Creating compelling copy is often ignored by email campaigners. There is a belief that incentivizing a customer is all you have to do to acquire them. This is not true. People are incentivized more by magical words than concrete bargains. This may seem like a paradox but creating compelling copy is perhaps the greatest challenge you will face in email marketing. Your copy should also be consistent with your brand image. Your job does not end with creating an effective email. You also have to carefully plan where the email recipient would land on your website by clicking on a particular link.

Email marketing is an integral part of internet marketing. It is a challenge as well as an opportunity to reach out to customers.

Chapter 11- Viral marketing

What does viral marketing mean and why is it important to create viral content? Viral means spreading your content in a geometric proportion in such a way that it attracts massive traffic to your website. Imagine how a virus spreads in a computer network? Like the ILOVEYOU virus? This is the tremendous power of viral marketing.

Harnessing the power of viral marketing does not require knowledge of rocket science. Once you understand the basics you can create content which will spread like a wildfire. You should remember one thing – going viral is not the end but a beginning. You must benefit for it and not merely create waves in the online space.

Now the first step in creating viral content is to imagine how gossip is transmitted in a group. Gossip means idle talk about private affairs of others (especially in their absence) without confirming its truth or veracity. Gossip is juicy content with spicy details about an event related to a person known to the parties involved with it. Not that you should convert your website into a gossip column. Far from it. You must learn lessons from gossip and convert them into interesting ideas which would attract customers.

In the context of internet marketing viral content usually takes the form of videos, online games and shocking but truthful news. Ask this question to yourself – What kind of content I will pass on to my friends and coworkers? Or better – what kind of content do I usually like to share with others? It is possible that you may have to go a bit beyond your normal spiel to make your content really viral. The best part is that you can pick up an idea from the internet and modify it to suit your requirements.

Viral marketing consists of three distinct stages. The first, of course, is the creation of content itself. The message should be short and to the point. People lose interest when you provide stuff which is long and yawn-ful. Videos should not be longer than fifteen seconds unless they can hold the attention of the viewer. Do not test the patience of your customer. Do not expect your content, even if it goes viral, to convert into instant customers. Publicity and exposure are important objectives which you must target.

The second part of viral marketing is to smartly insert your content into viral channels. You may have a happening Facebook profile with a few hundred friends. This number of friends is more than enough to make your message go viral. Imagine that only a hundred among your Facebook friends share your content. These shares will spawn fifty shares each, which means total shares of 50x100 adding upto 5000 shares. Now, your content is shared by fifty percent – 2500x 50 = 125000 share and so on. Get the idea? This is viral marketing.

Your job does not end here. You should track all the shares and monitor the progress of your original content. You will realize that your message has spread like a………virus. You would have built a loyal group of followers in a just a few days' time.

Emails as a viral channel

Emails are a great medium to spread your message and making it viral. In addition to creating unique and captivating content, you must provide additional enticement or incentive to make them share the email. A small gift can work wonders. You can give away an ebook free if your target audience shares the content. The viral nature of the emails becomes obvious when you see their multiplication effect. For ensuring that people share your emails, you must first identify your target audience. For example, let's assume that you have a free giveaway which talks about 'Five guaranteed ways to get published'. Your target audience comprising of writers can be reached by approaching them via websites dedicated to writers and publishers. Once you seed your content into emails and add the free gift, you can expect your mail to go viral. You can even ask the readers to subscribe to your newsletters to get access to the free gift.

You would have noticed that there is an overwhelming call for action from your audience. You have to compel them to share your content and this can best be achieved through provided incentives.

PR sites as viral channels

PR sites have a huge audience who consume a humungous amount of news. Do you have something newsworthy to say? If yes, you can seed your content in PR sites and expect thousands of views. You can direct the readers to your website and convert them into permanent visitors. You should be creative and write newsworthy content even if you have nothing much to say. In fact, news has to be created and does not fall into your lap often. You can piggy back on some other newsworthy article online. For example, you can sell your 100% waterproof raincoats by placing alongside news regarding a hurricane. By doing this you have a ready consumer in need of your product.

Facebook and Twitter

Facebook and twitter are the best viral agents among social media sites. A tweet can change opinions of millions of people. Even the President of United States has taken to Twitter vouching for its impact. Twitter is designed in such a way that it is easy to share via retweets. The best part is that you don't have to sweat much to write a tweet – only 140 characters. You should make sure that you have something funny or interesting to say in your tweet. You should not expect customers to drop in because of your tweets. Use the medium judiciously and take a long term approach. Tweets can be fun and highly rewarding if you can be a bit creative. Viral marketing and Twitter go hand in hand – they are made for each other.

Facebook is another viral medium with infinite potential, especially if your target audience is young. Facebook users share posts if they find it interesting or useful. Jokes can run havoc on Facebook. You should create suitable graphics and images to attract readers. You can sell almost anything if you are smart and creative.

Viral marketing is the ultimate in internet marketing. You are sure to become an addict once you get a taste for viral marketing.

Chapter 12 - Social media marketing

Social media marketing is an important part of internet marketing. The influence of Facebook, Twitter, and Instagram etc. has been growing steadily over the years. Social media is no longer only fun but a serious business. Your strategy should be to integrate all the features of social media seamlessly into internet marketing. The message should be uniform and clear. There is a mistaken belief that social media platforms should be a standalone activity. You must understand that the purpose of social media is different. These sites should be used to gather prospects and for feeding into the sales funnel. They act as influencers putting subtle psychological pressure on readers by creating a positive image. The impact on readers and prospects would be greater if you don't start selling right away on social media. People will tend to ignore your message thinking that you are trying to sell something. They will treat it like a promotion or an advertisement. Don't let your prospects feel that you are selling (which you are by the way). Provide great content which people like to read about. Associate your content with memorable events. Can you connect the news with your message? People like to read about hot and happening events. Creating content which revolves around current events will fetch you eyeballs.

Facebook marketing

On Facebook you are dealing with a new currency – likes and shares. Just because you have a personal account on Facebook on which you post a selfie does not mean you know everything about Facebook. There are two distinct parts on Facebook. You are already aware of the first (on which you post a selfie). The second part is the one which is meant for business. This is called the Facebook page. You can create a Facebook page free of cost, but what should you post in it? This is the moment to think of your overall internet marketing strategy.

What do you want to achieve from your Facebook page? You will find that people are selling stuff on Facebook. Good for them. In fact, Facebook claims that it is a great place to sell your stuff. However, people don't come to Facebook to buy anything. What do they come here for? To have fun, play games and showoff their selfie. What do you think will happen if you thrust your product on their face? They will run away from you.

Now, change your strategy a bit. Use the Facebook page to provide interesting information. Maybe a post on health benefits of Facebook? Creating curiosity and interest should be your first priority. This place is to create awareness. The real selling must be done on your website. Use Facebook for lead generation and do it subtly.

Facebook is an excellent platform for viral marketing. The 'share' button can get you a million clicks in a day – no kidding. But why would anyone like to share your post? Think about it and you will get the answer.

Twitter marketing

A tweet is worth a thousand words. You can gauge the popularity of Twitter from the fact even the President of America uses it to announce internationally important events. Twitter is the perfect tool to announce discounts, offers, attractions, rebates, bargains and deals. With the right words, your message has the power to spread like a wildfire. Building a Twitter strategy makes perfect sense. Internet marketing is all about sharing and twitter does it in less than 140 characters. You must remember that Twitter alone will not be of much help. You must use other social media like Facebook to build your online persona. Twitter is for instant news, current events …………..stuff which is happening now, right off the oven.

Bookmarking

Bookmarking sites like Reddit, Stumbleupon, Delicious and Pinterest attract a huge number of visitors. Consumers with varied interests look up these sites seeking information in specific areas. You must have an account on all these platforms to spread the good word. These bookmarking sites are known hangouts for creating viral messages. You never know – you might hit the lottery and attract a huge number of visitors thanks to these sites. Creating your profile on these sites is easy but to maintain constant visibility needs attention. You have to be active on these sites and update information at least once a week. It takes months to build a good presence but it is certainly worth the effort.

Internet business has now gone mobile. Consumers are looking for instant discounts and lap offers which are meaningful. Social media marketing must be used proactively to reap a rich harvest.

Conclusion

Here is the biggest secret to succeed in internet marketing ....there is no secret. There is no secret sauce. The internet is an open forum and no one controls it. Moreover, most of the activities on the internet are free. Of course, you have to put tremendous effort to make millions but the best part is that you can do it without investing an enormous amount of money.

The focus of this book has been mostly on using your copywriting skills to master internet marketing. You were exposed to designing effective websites with the sole aim to attract, retain, influence and persuade a visitor to click on the buy button.

The internet has once again made it clear that customer is king. The entire purpose of internet marketing is to locate, attract and compel customers to but your product or service. The nature of marketing does not change whether you are into traditional markets or selling online.

Understanding the customer is your primary and most important need. Who is your target customer? What does he or she want from you? What do they look like or what is their behavior like? These are questions which must be satisfactorily answered if you wish to succeed in internet marketing.

Copywriting skills are critical to your internet marketing effort. What goes into making a good copy must concern you the most. Digital does not mean speaking in machine language. Buyers are still human and they want to read legible words which are meaningful. This means you must speak to the buyer in terms of his needs and wants – not merely offer discount coupons. Effective copywriting should convince the reader about the elements which appeal emotionally to him or her. In the end, your product is only as good as your copy. Fantastic products fail because they are not marketed properly and poor products sell like crazy because of the copy.

You have no option but to create the perfect sales page. What this mean is that you have to tailor the message according to your product. Each landing page is unique and specific to your product.

'Swipe files' make you write fabulous copy without sweating it out. Everyone learns from the masters. Every internet marketer requires a 'swipe file' which they can use to create incredible impact. A swipe file is an essential part of a copywriter's toolkit. You can create impactful and highly effective content using swipe files. Swiping is not plagiarism because you are not copying the actual words but only the idea and concept. Learn about the structure, flow and control from masters of this art and do what has already been done – but differently. You have learnt the secret of creating 'swipe files' in this book and now it is time for you to get the creative juices flowing.

You leant about sales funnel in this book. This concept is critical for success on the internet. A sales funnel is only as good as your internet marketing strategy. Don't get stuck with three step or five step sales funnel. Be creative and look at the big picture. Let your prospects get magnetically attracted to your product. Create sales funnel which would be impossible to ignore. Let the consumers fall gently into your lap. There is no need to push and hustle your prospect.

Affiliate marketing has changed the way we do business. It is one of the defining aspects of internet marketing. Imagine a salesperson on hormones! Imagine someone getting rich without investing much upfront! Imagine democratization of wealth! Affiliate marketing is all this and more. Affiliate marketing has opened up opportunities for millions of people who could not afford to invest huge amount of money in business. Grab this opportunity with both your hands. Embrace affiliate marketing. There are millions of affiliate opportunities online. Just spend some time understanding the concept and you will not regret it.

Email marketing is not dead. Many of you must already have discarded this tool in favor of some other exotic strategy. Don't. Email marketing is still a powerful tool to discover new prospects and to keep active customers engaged. Internet marketers must create suitable strategies to deploy this handy and useful tool to boost customer base and enable effective customer retention.

What does viral marketing mean and why is it important to create viral content? Viral means spreading your content in a geometric proportion in such a way that it attracts massive traffic to your website. Harnessing the power of viral marketing does not require knowledge of rocket science. Once you understand the basics you can create content which will spread like a wildfire.

Social media has become a major part of internet marketing. Facebook has the power to mold consumer perceptions can create new and powerful ways to market your product and services. On Facebook you are dealing with a new currency – likes and shares. Create strategies to convert 'likes' and 'shares' into 'buys'. Use social media to attract buyers to your sales funnel. Social media as a marketing tool is still evolving. Savvy marketers are experimenting with this media. The best part is that no one can control social media and there is no fear that it will be purchased by a powerful media mogul and exploited exclusively by them.

Internet marketing is a whole new game which is open to everyone. No one owns it and no one has exclusive rights to it or will ever have. The opportunities are immense as long as you know how to create strategies to harness its power. You need new and novel ideas to take your internet marketing effort to a higher level.

Follow the techniques which have been explained in this book and you will soon master internet marketing. Remember that there is no end to learning. Don't think that you can rest after reading this book. Keep exploring. Keep your eyes and ears open. Be receptive to novel concepts and ideas. The new world is yours to enjoy and profit from. Go for it.